I0197554

Thriving After Divorce

Mary Olufunmilayo Adekson

NHP

Copyright © 2020 by Mary Olufunmilayo Adekson

All rights reserved. No part of this publication may be reproduced, distributed or transmitted in any form or by any means, including photocopying, recording, or other electronic or mechanical methods, without the prior written permission of the publisher, except in the case of brief quotations embodied in critical reviews and certain other noncommercial uses permitted by copyright law. For permission requests, write to the publisher, addressed "Attention: Permissions Coordinator," at the address below.

Adekson/New Harbor Press
1601 Mt. Rushmore Rd, Ste 3288
Rapid City, SD 57701
www.newharborpress.com

Thriving After Divorce/Mary Olufunmilayo Adekson —1st ed.
ISBN 978-1-63357-360-4

Dedication

THRIVING AFTER DIVORCE IS first dedicated to God Almighty who makes "the stone which the builders rejected (to) become the chief cornerstone" of the house (Psalm 118:22). Lord, what you do with broken lives is marvelous in our eyes. Jeremiah 18 verse 4 says, a broken life can be made beautiful when it is touched by God's love and grace.

Thriving after Divorce is also dedicated to all those who have gone through the sufferings and perils of divorce and survived and also to those who will go through divorce and survive by God's grace.

And also, to all the children of divorce all over the world.

Standing on the promises that cannot fail
When the howling storms of doubt and fear assail,
By the living Word of God, I shall prevail,
Standing on the promises of God
--Carter
When we are weak and in despair,
Our mighty God is near;
He'll give us strength and joy and hope,
And calm our inner fear
---Sper

Contents

Who is Mary Olufunmilayo Adekson?

MY CHILDHOOD WAS FULL of spiritual adventures after I accepted the Lord Jesus Christ as my Lord and Savior when I was 8 years old. My life has not been the same ever since I encountered my Lord. I remember clinging tightly to the beautiful picture of the lilies (Matthew 6:28-30) that my Sunday School Teacher gave us after her sermon to us about God's provision and care, that unforgettable and divine Sunday. I determined and resolved in my heart to love this Almighty Father who takes care of the lilies in the field which are here today and destroyed tomorrow. I possessed a childlike belief that this God is going to take care of me throughout my life here on earth. The rest is history. I was transformed with a dramatic vision of God with a personal relationship with Him and God has proved Himself to me over all these years and He still continues to deliver on His Promises. I go to Him for answers for all situations in my life. He listens and answers my cries, petitions and prayers. I am also grateful to my Godly earthly father, late Papa Gabriel Omodele Ekundiya Asanbe-Williams who stood by me during trials, troubles and tribulations. As Psalm 112 verse 6b says, "The righteous shall be in everlasting remembrance." You are remembered for all your fatherly care for me and my family.

I am a walking miracle because of Jesus Christ who loves me. I am grateful to You God for the opportunity to know You and be a living witness for You. I stand ! I stand in awe of You !! Holy God to whom all praise is due !!! I stand in awe of You !!!! Thank you so much God. You are AWESOME, HOLY, EXCELLENT and GREAT !!!!!

Introduction

TO TELL YOU THE truth I am not advocating for divorce in anybody's life because God hates divorce because of the breaking of convenant (tearing of flesh) and for what it does to the children (Malachi 2:16). But when divorce happens, as it does happen, God loves divorcees because they are broken-hearted (Psalm 34:18) and they look up to Him for love and guidance. Confidence happens because of a mate's assurance of love, loyalty and fidelity. Unfortunately, these promises are broken because of human frailty and sin. And divorce happens whether we like it or not. We live in a broken world and we are human beings. As Cindy Hess Kasper of Our Daily Bread Ministries encouraged, "we are never too badly broken for God to reshape. He loves us in spite of our imperfections and past mistakes, and He desires to make us beautiful." A lot has been written about divorce. But I am looking at divorce from a professional and Biblical point of view in *Thriving After Divorce*. So, take cover. Get a blanket and snuggle with your children if you have any, or in front of your fireplace if it's winter or stay warm in the embrace of Jesus Christ who came to the world and suffered for us all. You are in for a treat.

The "D" word: devastating, dehumanizing, dreaded, like a limb cut off and more.

DIVORCE IS HARD. IT is like going to school again and sweating for grades and waiting to make sure you pass the test. The test of adversity. I labelled it the "D" word. Devastating, dehumanizing, dreaded and it leaves you feeling as if one of your limbs has been cut off. This is especially true if you are the one on the receiving end. That is, the one who did not initiate the divorce. Even if you are not the one who initiated the divorce, you will still be affected because there was once a glimpse of love when you got married in the first place. But for a child of God, after all the turmoils and go-arounds, there is light at the end of the tunnel if you can rely on your Papa who brought you here. God sees all things and knows all things. He knows the end from the beginning. He knows you, He crafted you in your Mama's womb, and He says you are fearfully and wonderfully made (Psalm 139:14). All hope is not lost. And as David Egner of Our Daily Bread Ministries pointed out, "when the turbulent seas of adversity are threatening, we need to remember the awesome power of God." And remember, "pain and problems can produce the shining rock-solid character that comes from trusting God when life is hard" (Jennifer Benson Schuldt, Our Daily Bread Ministries). Rock-solid character comes shining from trusting God in the face of adversity. If all those who are divorced can stand tall today, believe me, my sister and brother you will stand tall very, very soon and tell others of God's goodness, mercy and grace. The stone which has been rejected obviously becomes the chief cornerstone (Psalm 118:22). Just believe and don't take your eyes from looking at your Savior Jesus Christ. Turn your eyes upon Jesus.... and the things of earth (world) will grow (faintly) and strangely dim in the light of His glory and grace. "But my eyes are on You, O God the Lord; In You I take refuge" (Psalm 141:8). You know what: God "will keep you in perfect peace" because your mind is stayed on Him and because you trust in Him (Isaiah 26:3). Put all your **total** trust in Him during this trying-times, and you will be vindicated and encouraged if you are wronged. Heed God's Words in Romans 12 verse 19 that says: "beloved, do not avenge yourselves, but rather give place to wrath; for it is written, vengeance is mine I will repay says the Lord." Be still and know that God is God (Psalm 46:10). Do not view the other person as your enemy. Leave God to be the judge because He knows and sees all things. It's easier said than done, but it works if you can be still and let go and let God take the steering wheel of your life during this time and throughout the rest of your life. Romans 12 verse 21 concludes that we "not be overcome by evil but overcome evil with good." Pray for wisdom and discernment as you think deeply about these Godly pieces of advice. God will lead you to have a Christ-like attitude and mind during these cloudy moments. Whatever side you are on, God sees your heart because He knows exactly what transpires during and after your marriage. Let Him take care of things for you and your children. As the first half in a game does not determine the outcome of the game, be assured that since you are still here on earth, your life is worth more that this sudden failure or disappointment. Remember, God has another plan. And He will perfect all those things that concerns you (Psalm 138:8a), and He will make all things work together for good for you (Romans 8:28). Like Paul said in Philippians 3 verses 13 to 14 look to the future forget the past and trust in your Papa who can do all things. He will neither leave you nor forsake you (Deuteronomy 31: 6 & 8; Joshua 1:5; Hebrews 13:5). God will not leave you as an orphan. He will be your comforting Father.

Coping with divorce

GOD'S GOODNESS IS EVIDENT in God's relationship with His children whom He adoringly loves (Nahum 1:7; Daniel 1; Psalm 119:49-50; Hebrews 13:5). When it's just you and God that's enough. "The future always looks bright when viewed through the window of God's promises" and "With God behind you and His arms beneath you, you can face whatever is before you" (Dave Branon, Our Daily Bread Ministries). It is very hard to realize that all the dreams you have "for better for worse until death do us part,' has suddenly come crashing down on your head. Where is all that love gone? Well, things happen. Human beings are all born into sin. Yes, the sin of Adam. But God will assist and help when things turn out sour. This was why He sent His only begotten Son to come and save us because "many are the afflictions of the righteous, but the Lord delivers (her or) him out of them all" (Psalm 34:19). As I reiterated in the previous chapter, there is light at the end of the tunnel. How do we get to the end? Through perseverance and putting our total trust in God. Yes, in God Almighty who rights all wrongs. James said we should count it all joy when we fall into various trials and tribulations because they work in us for the better (James 1:2-4;

Romans 5:3-4). The Lord will eventually "restore to you the years that the swarming locust has eaten" (Joel 2:25a). "Adversity is part of the process that God uses to produce good results in our lives. "Trouble, if it turns us to the Lord, could actually be the best thing for us. It leaves us wholly dependent on Him (and) God uses our difficulties to develop our character" (David H. Roper, Our Daily Bread Ministries). Pray for grace in the midst of afflictions (James 1:2-4; Romans 5:3-4). So, stand firm and rely on your Father. Hold on to your confidence of hope because God has promised, and He is faithful (Hebrews 10:23). Surrender totally to God. Do not give in to despair or defeat. Like David, do not give in to defeat, but ask God for a strategy and turn to God for strength to recover all (1 Samuel 30:6&8) as you surrender and cope. Ruminate on the Word of God and pray. God sees you. God knows you. God hears you. He sees the feelings of shame, insecurities and worthlessness that pervade in your life right now. Just look to Jesus, the author and finisher of your faith. Fellowship with ardent believers who do not judge you. Remain faithful to God and your Savior. You need to know that someone loves you, that you are worthwhile, and that your life count for something in the world. A solid relationship in Jesus Christ will proffer this knowledge and help you solidify your worth as His friend, sister and brother and as God's child (Ephesians 5:21-6:4; Genesis 25:21-23; Psalm 139:13; Jeremiah 1:4-5). God is always making things right on His children's behalf (John 3:16; Romans 8:31b-32). God's grace gives you hope not only for today but for all eternity. God will help you go through hard circumstances even when you have no idea how to endure (Philippians 4:7). He can assist you through His wisdom, power and strength to work through the obstacles and problems of divorce and its aftermath. The Lord has not forgotten you. So, approach each day as a present from God (Proverbs 17:22). Take one day at a time relying on your Papa to see you through the sadness and loneliness of this time. Know that God is in perfect control and that He will direct your steps as He promised in His Word. He will work everything together for your good (Romans 8:28). Though you can feel lonely at this time, know that Jesus will be your companion. He has felt as you are feeling now because He was also human, and He is able to comfort you during this ordeal and see you through. Trust God now that things have changed in your life. Don't fret. Don't worry. Cast away fear. The Lord will deliver you from all your fears (Psalm 34:4b). Stay on course with your Maker. He brought you here. He will see you through and use the situation for His glory in your life. Use the opportunity God allows in your life now to embrace a fresh new significance for every moment life gives you. Sper reiterated that "sometimes our plan does not unfold the way we thought it would, but God is always in control to use it for our good." God is the Director of your life. Everything will turn out right. If you put your whole trust in God, you will look back and praise Him for the lean years and for seeing you through your times of agony and distress. When you put your trust in God, He will set you apart and give you favor. For the Lord set apart for Himself those that are Godly and hear when you call to Him in your pain and hurt (Psalm 4:3). And in your distress cry to the Lord, and He will hear you (Psalm 120:1). Yes, He will. You will come out as a better, mature well-equipped child of God. The Hand of the Lord will be upon you and your children if you have children. God will never leave you nor forsake you (Deuteronomy 31:6&8). Do not be afraid He will be with you for He is your God (Isaiah 41:10) and He is your refuge and strength an ever-present help in trouble (Psalm 46:1). Yes, an ever present help, as you go through the court papers, get a lawyer, look for money to pay all the costs. Hold your head up. Look towards your Papa for where the money is going to come from and for strength to cope through the court ordeal. The Lord shall supply all your needs according to His riches in glory in Christ Jesus (Philippians 4:19). Yes, He will see you through with few cheerleaders, and more critics all around you. Hold your head high despite all that the nay-sayers may be saying. Pray. Read the Word. Eat well and exercise. Believe God. Take care of your physical, spiritual and emotional needs. Heed Paul's advice to the Thessalonians that says: "that you also aspire to lead a quiet life, to mind your own business, and to work with your own hands as we command you" (1 Thessalonians 4:11). You will come out victorious. It is not going to be easy. But "little by little" (Exodus 23:30), you shall overcome all obstacles in your way. God says to you like He said to Jeremiah: "for I will surely deliver you, and you shall ...., but your life shall be a prize to you because you have put your trust in Me says the Lord" (Jeremiah 39:18). Believe me, you will smile and sing God's praise in the end if you put your **whole** trust in Him. For when you hope in the Lord, He will give you mercy and you will have abundant redemption, and He will redeem you from all your iniquities (Psalm 130:7&8). You are under grace today, and you will be under grace tomorrow. The past cannot hurt you, and the future cannot overcome you. No matter what is going on in your life now or what will transpire in the future, the Lord is saying to you as He said to Joshua: "have I not commanded you? Be strong and of good courage do not be afraid nor be dismayed, for the Lord your God is with you wherever you go" (Joshua 1:9). Let Brandt words: "onward and upward your course plan today, seeking new heights as you walk Jesus' way; heed not just failures, but strive for the prize, aiming for goals fit for His holy eyes," encourage you today. Begin again with God who turns failures into successes. Our God who encourages you, will heed you to keep going in the midst of afflictions because "many are the afflictions of the righteous, but the Lord delivers us from all of them (Psalm 34:19). Turn to God now as you face intense disappointments, hurts, challenges and temptations. Seek the Lord while He may be found, call upon Him while He is near (Isaiah 55:6). Be closer to God. Draw close to God and He will draw closer to you in this your time of need.

You should always be inclined to say that, "God's unseen presence comforts me I know He is always near; and when life's storms besiege my soul, He says, 'My child I am here" (Dennis J. DeHaan, Our Daily Bread Ministries). Pray for protection, strength and courage for yourself and your child or children (Philippians 4:6). God, who is your Heavenly Father, who knows and loves you more than anyone else could, is there and will be there for you. Again, I say, be prayerful. Turn your anxiety and fears over to God. Pour out your cries and your concerns to God and hope for the best from the Lord who genuinely loves you and your seeds. He will give you wisdom to navigate this ordeal and give you guidance as you raise your children or work through your pains alone if you do not have a child. This chaos, shame and obstacles shall become your messages of hope for those coming behind. Yes, you will have a testimony to help and assist others after this too has passed. Let God be the Master of your life from now on. You will not be disappointed. Believe me, you will stand tall. As you face shock, shame, loss and hurt, turn to the One who brought you here in the first place (Psalm 139) and you will not be ashamed. All those feelings will be replaced with joy after you navigate all the pains and sorrows of divorce. The joy of the Lord will be your strength (Nehemiah 8:10). Then you will be able to sing of His praise and His mercy in the morning because He has been your defense and refuge in the day of your trouble (Psalm 59:16c). Your joy will become new every morning because great is His faithfulness (Lamentations 3:23). And even if He causes grief, He will have compassion according to the multitude of His mercies for He does not willingly grieve us His children (Lamentations 3:32-33). Oswald Chambers reiterated that, "Jesus Christ says that ultimately through patience and by deliberately going on with God, everything that is now obscure will be clear....... If we 'hang in' with patience, we shall see everything rehabilitated, and God will be justified in everything He has allowed." Hold on to your confession of hope because

God who has promised is faithful (Hebrews 10:23). God will ultimately give you resilience, supply you with joy and all the resources you need to succeed. God loves you and He wants to bless every area of your life. Turn to God when you face intense disappointments, hurts, temptations and challenges. Go to God for strength, protection, hope and courage for yourself and your children and be anxious about nothing (Philippians 4:6). God is your heavenly Father who loves you more than anyone else could. I say it again: Be prayerful. Turn your fears and anxiety over to God Almighty. Pour out your cries and hold your concerns up to God. Hope for the best from the Lord who is your Father who sees and knows your heart. Yes, there has been failure in your life. But know one thing, God defines you (Isaiah 14:27), not the failure in your life. And no one can redirect the plan that God your Father has ordained for you. God accepts you because He made you in His own image fearfully and wonderfully (Romans 8:1; Psalm 139:14). God will lift you up if you go to Him when you fail. You will not be abandoned if you abandon yourself to the Almighty God as you go through this tribulation. Your destiny is with God who brought you here. Be faithful even during this time of sorrow. Keep serving the Lord and looking up to Him for the resolution of all the problems and challenges you are facing right now. You will have cause to glorify His Name in the end. You will have a testimony that comes out of this test and a message and order out of this mess and chaos. The more you trust God, the more you will realize that God is excellent all the time. The Lord exudes love, mercy, grace, abundance, forgiveness, joy, contentment, gentleness, and patience towards His children. As a father pities his children, so the Lord pities them those who fear Him (Psalm 103:13). The Lord, your Shepherd, will be with you and give you all you need (Psalm 23). All you have to do during this difficult time is to ask Him for your needs, to help restore your strength, guide you along the right paths and assist you to bring honor to His Name. You need to look up to your Father as He reassures you and hold you up when you are down and help you to regain your equilibrium and balance in life. He will help you as you smile again and get your confidence, joy and strength back. Jesus is there for you when you feel hopeless and helpless and without comfort. Call on Him and confide in Him as your best friend. Rely on God for your provision (Genesis 22:14; Philippians 4:19); for your healing and restoration (Isaiah 53:4-5; Psalm 103:3; Psalm 23:3) for your peace of mind (Judges 6:24) and for your completeness, trustworthiness, happiness (Isaiah 26:3). Lean on the Holy Spirit to take your further than you imagine and make impossibles possible in your life. The Holy Spirit will turn your sad past into joyous present and future and you will be victorious. Oswald Chambers encouraged us that, "whenever there are competing concerns in your life, be sure you always put your relationship to God first." **Thrive** in the bosom of your Father. Leave the uncertainties to God. He will make your uncertainties become certain. Leave all your concerns at the foot of the cross. Remember that, "there is an Arm that never tires when human strength gives way; (and) there is a Love that never fails when earthly loves decay" (Wallace). The fact that God proclaims that, "I am the Lord, I do not change" (Malachi 3:6), should strengthen us and give us confident backbone in the face of our trials, difficulties and examinations and assure us of God's ability to fulfill His divine promise. Because of His unchanging love and presence, we "are not consumed" (Malachi 3:6). And we can draw on His compassion which are "new every morning" (Lamentations 3:22-23). Our God---- The Faithful God of love will stay with us in our trials and tribulations. May God restore your confidence, joy and strength (Psalm 23), when you feel helpless and hopeless. Amen. God will guide, support and lift you up in Jesus' Name. Amen.

Raising your children in the fear of the Lord

GOD INSTRUCTED US IN Psalm 78 verses 5 to 6 to teach our children to honor and respect God. Have a Godly response to your afflictions (2 Corinthians 4:17; Romans 8:18; Psalm 34:19; 38:9; 86:7). "The power of God within you is greater than the pressure of troubles around you" (David Egner, Our Daily Bread Ministries). Look up to God as you train your children. Look up, look up, don't be frightened, the Savior understands it will be well. Proverbs 22 verse 6 says "train up a child in the way he (or she) should go and when (she or) he is old he (or she) will not depart from it." Let me assure you that training them up in the way is not going to be easy because you have so many disadvantages crawling around as you do this. Maybe one of them is an unsaved former spouse and his or her relatives and friends or even her or his new husband or wife. Another enemy is anger in your children. Children of divorce have lots of bottled anger within them that they unleash on their parents from time to time. Pray with them as they navigate the confusion and anger related to separation and divorce. Read the Word to them daily.

Shower them with love. Let them know that God loves them and tell them He has not abandoned them. Lead by example in your words and actions. Train and discipline them (Proverbs 22:6). Do not be afraid to lead and correct them and let them know rights from wrongs. The devil and the world are also culprits too. But be of good cheer you have overcome the world as Jesus did (John 16:33). In the world you will have tribulation but be of good cheer you and your children have overcome the world (John 16:33). But do not relent, if you have God on your side the battle is won. Although the children may wander, they will come back to the Lord if you persistently continue to feed them with the Word of God and pray over them. Lead by example. Do not do anything that you advice your children against. Give them Biblical examples to infuse Godly character into them. Believe me it works on the long run. Attend a solid Bible believing Church where they will come in contact with Godly individuals who are living Godly lives. God will heal you and your children from hurt, bitterness and anger. Be a Godly parent: spiritually and physically. Encourage your children. And that means, those that we give birth to physically, spiritually or through adoption. Paul encouraged Timothy and brought him up in the fear and admonition of the Lord (1 Timothy 1:2). So, do the same for your children. Do not grieve your children. Love them and discipline them, believe in them and cheer them on in the battle of life. Train them up in the fear and admonition of the Lord and when they are old, they will not depart from God's way (Proverbs 22:6). So, "do not withhold correction from a child. For if you beat him (or her) with a rod, he (or she) will not die" (Proverbs 23:13). Correct your child. Speak wisdom into their ears and hearts. Teach and imbibe into them the Word of God (Deuteronomy 6:5-9) and assist them to put their life experiences into proper perspectives, leave their comfort zones and take risks. You can do this by listening to them and giving them Godly advice and offer them options to grow. There are times when children wander like the prodigal. Be assured that the Word of God and the Spirit of God will find them and redirect them to refocus. Let there be boundaries and teach them the fear and admonition of the Lord. Help them as they inculcate Godly values and principles. Take time to nurture, care and provide for both their physical, emotional, mental and spiritual needs. Love them genuinely as God loves you. Do not abuse them or use languages that are ungodly. As Moses told the Israelites, pass the Godly touch to them as the next generation. Then you can say like Joshua said: As for me and my house we will serve the Lord (Joshua 24:15c). Remember one thing, as we humbly walk with our Savior and rely on His strength, He will empower us to accomplish what's only possible through Him like He did with Gideon (Judges 6:14). So, plod on and persevere. God's strength and power will see you through and help you perform your parental duties during this troubled period. Lead your children to the Lord at a tender age. Teach them the fear, admonition and ways of the Lord early and when they are old, they will not depart from the Lord's way. Constantly check on your children's spiritual growth in the Lord from time to time. Encourage, teach, direct, instruct and admonish. Be a good example in word and actions as you use the Word of the Bible as precepts in your teachings and daily interactions. Help them grow and flourish in the Lord all their lives and you would have left a lasting heritage as God instructed the Israelites to do for their children. Discourage and direct them not to be unequally yoked with unbelievers. Give them room to grow in the Lord and in their lives. Instill words of wisdom into their lives by encouraging them to read the Word of God and through proverbs, wise sayings and from archives of experience. Encourage them to tap into their God-given resources and talents and abilities to help other citizens of the world. Instill confidence into their lives. Help them develop Godly character and integrity. Watch them grow in the fear and admonition of the Lord. Please note that educational achievements without instilling the fear of the Lord with Godly characteristics is useless. Imbibe in them that following the Lord is the best and only way to live a successful life forever. Lloyd George, a former British Prime Minister reiterated that "education without God makes clever devils." Only the inspiration of God's Word into a child's life can make them live life well and to the full. Make sure you love them equally and pray for wisdom to avoid favoritism. Be sensitive to each of your children's needs. Being a parent is like being a steward and taking care of someone that God gave us to care for. We are not the owners of those children God has commissioned us to care for. Because, before God made our children, He knew them and commissioned them for great things like He informed Jeremiah and David (Jeremiah 1:5-9; Psalm 139:13). They were created for a Godly purpose and have a destiny that has been designed solely by the Almighty. We should therefore look to God to help us do the job He has entrusted to us. It is an assignment. We should be prayerful as we nurture, guide and teach and direct the young ones through life. God always helps. He is able. Dedicate them to the Lord at a young age and release them to God when it is time for them to fly like the eaglet that is let out of the nest. Do not play God in your children's lives. Refrain from being the Director of the Universe or Amateur Providence in their lives. Allow God to be the God of their lives. Give them room to grow as God's child.

Co-parenting in Godly ways

THIS IS A VERY important part where you have split custody of the children. The children now have to shuttle between two homes and at times two different ideologies and principles. As I wrote in the last chapter, train up your child to fear the Lord. Do not speak badly about anyone to your children even when they come back home to you with differenst stories from their weekend or time with the other spouse and their family members. Keep communication open because of the children and for your sanity. Bite your tongue. Avoid arguing and fighting in front of the children. Let sleeping dog lie. Let bygone be bygone. Let go and let God. Speak to your children honestly about what is transpiring between you and your ex-spouse. Do not hide under any façade. Be honest and help them deal with the anger and emotions through prayer and by instilling the Word of God into their lives. Say some prayers every day that God help you keep to this delicate principle. Know one thing. The children are smart. They will figure everything out in the end and identify everyone's character. So do not ruin their chance of finding out who and what everyone is or does by offering your opinion about others to them. Children learn about their parents in due time driven by their curiosity and intelligence. Eventually they will make up their minds about each parent over time. Continue to train them in the way of the Lord. Cover them with the blood of Jesus and pray over them as they move from abode to abode. Believe me, God will not let any evil befall them. Also look out for abuse and report it if your children tell you about any. Be careful to get all the facts straight and do not dispel what they tell you. Take them seriously. This too shall pass. God will protect them, and they will grow up stronger during and after this ordeal. Do not let your gird down. Pray, fast if you can, and lift everyone up to the Lord. Remember, God loves all of you and Jesus died for all of you. All things will work out well for all of you in the end (Romans 8:28) and our God shall perfect all that concerns all of you (Psalm 138:8a).

And to you: children of divorce

THIS IS A DIFFICULT time for you ! But this too shall pass. Do not think that God does not love you because of what transpired between your parents. God is the Father to the fatherless (and motherless) as the case may be (Psalm 68:5-6). God loves you dearly and wants you to be a success in the world. You are not "less than." You are precious in His sight. God has a special place in His heart for you. You are special to Him. He sent His Son to the world because of you. God takes care of the broken-hearted. Jesus Christ is a light in your dark places now and a hope for you the confused, fearful, bitter, tensed, angry, comfortless, lonely, neglected and broken hearted. God will not leave you even though your parents are divorced. So, turn to Him at this critical time and throughout your life. Believe me, He cares, and He will not disappoint you. He will neither leave you nor forsake you (Deuteronomy 31:6 & 8). He is a good God who knows exactly what is going on. Turn your anger to God. Give it to Him. Where possible discuss your feelings with a Christian counselor and your Youth Pastor or your Pastor at your church.

Lay it out in the open. Do not keep it bottled in. This will help you heal. Do not take the anger out on your parents. Love your parents even when they are not doing the right thing, but keep a distance if there is abuse. Report abuse promptly and appropriately to the right person so it can be taken care of. Above all put on love which is the bond of perfection (Colossians 3:14). Work on moving forward to heal. And whatever you do in word or deed giving thanks to God the Father, do all in the name of our Lord Jesus Christ (Colossians 3:17). Although the divorce is not your fault you still need to work through the emotions and heal so you can live a wholistic life. This is the most difficult phase because you just want to forget all that has happened. Do not suppress your emotions. What you do not bring to the open will not heal. It will be like an untended wound. So, intentionally face the reality of all that happened. Do not give in to self-hatred or guilt. Do not recline on self-pity. Self-pity is of the devil. Don't wallow in it so you can be blessed and used by God. Do not look for love in the wrong places. Run to Jesus Christ. He loves you the children, and also your parents. Accept the Lord Jesus Christ as your Lord and Savior. Make Jesus Christ your best friend and lean on the God of compassion for help. His compassion fails not (Lamentations 3:22-23). They are new every morning. Say no to ungodliness and worldly and wicked values and pursue godliness, patience and gentleness (Titus 2:11-12; Proverbs 4:14-15; 1 Timothy 6:11). Know one thing your Father God says you are precious and honored in His sight and that He loves you (Isaiah 43:4). Hold yourself in high esteem as your Papa holds you. Have boundaries. Honor yourself. Pray for wisdom as you interact and deal with people. Be wise and gentle but have discernment too. Do not be fearful of rejection since you know God has not rejected you. Go where you are celebrated and respected not where you are tolerated. Live as a child of God and **thrive**, not exist in His bosom care. So, in your trauma and anger seek Him so you can eventually become a comforting witness to other children of divorce coming behind (2 Corinthians 1:4). He will heal, restore and strengthen you in your afflictions so you can be a shining light to others (Ephesians 5:8). Do not despair. Know that this too shall pass and if you put your head on God as the pillow of your life now, you will praise His Name later in life. Persevere and have faith in the Father who brought you here in the first place (Psalm 139). Give yourself time to heal totally physically, psychologically and emotionally. Be confident in His wisdom and His certainty that all will be well. Be like Timothy and rely on God's grace and learn and know the Holy Scriptures which will make you wise for salvation through faith which is in Christ Jesus (2 Timothy 3:15). The One who fearfully and wonderfully knit you together in your mother's womb (Psalm 139:14), will assist you as you look up to Him to heal you. Become stronger in broken places. It is Ernest Hemmingway who said that, "the world breaks everyone and afterward many are strong at the broken places." Be among those who God will use to help others. Look for other Godly children of divorce in your church and form a Christ-centered group where you can use the Word of God to encourage one another. Pray. Read the Word. Praise God. Rely on God the Father, God the Son and God the Holy Spirit. Walk in love in Jesus footsteps, the One who has come to give us life more abundantly (John 10:10). Love yourself and other children of God because God is love. Beware of looking for love in the wrong places. Love not the world. Love Jesus Christ and follow His teachings. You are loved by God. You are not a discard. Believe me, He will carry you and keep you and His face will shine upon you because He cherishes you. Jesus loves children as portrayed in how He dealt with them when He was on earth (Matthew 19:13; Mark 10:16; Luke 18:16). You, as God's child, was bought with a precious blood of the Lamb. Walk around with your head high. No matter what anyone says, you are a Masterpiece (Ephesians 2:10). You are so, so special. You are God's jewel (Malachi 3: 16-17; Zechariah 9:16). Let the confidence of God be in your life. Be confident in yourself and in your God-given abilities. Love God and extend the love to yourself. Love yourself and love others too. Even though you are not perfect, God loves you as you are. Positively esteem yourself. Know that you are precious in God's eyes as I wrote before. Jesus loves you and wants to be your friend. What a friend we have in Jesus all our cares and worries to share. Think positive thoughts about your life today and what it will be in the future. This will lead to positive actions in your daily interactions with people that you are around. Maintain a level-headed approach to travail now so you can be an excellent witness for Jesus to others in their own time of need as you mature and move on from your sufferings.

The other woman or man

ANOTHER MAJOR THING TO contend with is the other man or woman in your former spouse's life if she or he has one now. Face this too with prayer. Meditate on the Word of God that says that you are a gift of God and very special to God. Do not let anyone put you down or treat you like a second-rate individual. You are divorced but not discarded. There will be so many opinions from different individuals. Scan them and make sure you listen and hold on to the positives. This is the time you will know your true friends. Tread carefully with caution and wisdom. Bite you tongue most of the time. Use your tongue wisely because some individuals will just want to hear what you will say and relay it to your former spouse and their new-found love. Be careful what you say. Treat this other person with respect and love them as God loves you. Do not despise them as they are made in God's image as yourself. Remember, God will fight for you, just learn to keep your peace and be still and rely on God the vindicator (Romans 12:19; Isaiah 35:4). Do not judge. Leave the judgement to God Almighty who sees all our hearts. Remember, you are complete in Christ. In Him you have the fullness of God.

The family who takes sides ! Your own family and friends !!

YES, THIS IS A time that you will know those who really love you. Face reality. Be sincere with yourself. Be discerning and use wisdom. The Word of God says we should be as wise as serpents and at the same time be as gentle as the doves (Matthew 10:16). Use wise judgement as you navigate and listen to comments from all and sundry. Like I reiterated earlier, do not let what individuals say or are saying affect you. Remember, you and your children are God's special children. You are God's Masterpiece (Ephesians 2:10). You are God's jewel (Malachi 3:16-17; Zechariah 9:16). There will be criticisms, and judgements will be passed by some members of your family and friends who profess a holier than thou and self-righteous attitudes. This is a time to pray and hold tightly to God and love those who love you and also treat those who judge or say wrong things about you with respect and Godly love. Jesus said, forgive them Lord, for they do not know what they are doing (Luke 23:34). Forgive. Do not hold grudges. Focus on God to fight for you. Put all your energy on raising your children in the way of the Lord and serving God with your whole heart. Some family members and friends will be on your side. Cherish them and let them know you appreciate all their support. Use their support as resources to help you especially if they are Christians and God-fearing individuals like you. Even when they are not, show them respect. Remember one thing: you know your true friends and enemies in times of adversity. Be careful and prayerful when you communicate with those who do not show you love. Have boundaries and be wise. Pray to God to let you have the wisdom to recognize the friends and acquaintances you should choose and be with from this time on. God will lead you away from and help you steer clear of relationships that will lead you away from the path He has laid out for you and send Godly men and women into your paths daily. He will bless you with the right individuals who will be of help to you and your children. He is the Father and helper of the fatherless (Psalm 68:5; 10:14) and He takes care of those that are forsaken, downtrodden and needs help. God will be the Lord of all your relationships and show you which relationships are worth keeping at this time of your life (Proverbs 13:20) and those you should not keep. And as you pray, be cautious and careful. Look, listen and observe.

Love yourself ! Have a Godly response to your afflictions !!

SECOND CORINTHIANS 4 VERSE 17 says that we should not lose heart because we are growing in the Lord every minute. Because we are growing, we will keep on learning new things about the Lord and our journey here on earth. Romans 8 verse 18 also admonishes us that sufferings of this present time is nothing compared to the glory that will be revealed in us. Psalm 34 verse 19 says that, many are our afflictions, but our Lord delivers us from all of them. And as Oswald Chambers reiterated, "it is in the midst of anguish and terror that we realize who God is and the marvel of what He can do." Psalm 38 verse 9 brought out the fact that the Lord knows us intimately and that our sighing and desires are all before Him. Psalm 86 verse 7 proclaims that we will call on the Lord in the day of our trouble and He will answer us. Paul said that our present sufferings "are not worthy to be compared with the glory which shall be revealed" (Romans 8:18) in us after the trials and sufferings have passed. Such hope comes from being anchored in Jesus Christ, our Savior. Spafford sang that "When peace like a river attendeth my way, when sorrows like sea billows roll; whatever my lot, thou hast taught me to say, It is well, it is well with my soul." Yes, it is well with your soul. Whatever you are going through right now, have hope in God that it will be well with your soul. Hess reiterated that, "events may sometimes touch our lives with change and dire destruction, but God by grace can heal, restore, and bring reconstruction." Your confidence, security and serenity come from God. Yes, from the God of peace who is your hiding place. Love and receive yourself in the fires of sorrow, despair and suffering. Lean daily on God's grace and know that you are victorious in Jesus Christ. God knows everything you are going through and He knows everything that happens in your life. God knows you individually and He is El Roi the One who sees you (Genesis 16:13). You are never alone. "O yes, He cares---- I know He cares ! His heart is touched with my grief; when the days are weary, the long nights dreary, I know my Savior cares" (Graeff). Oswald Chambers said something that encourages me, and I know it will encourage you too. He reiterated that, "if God can accomplish His purposes in this world through a broken heart, then why not thank Him for breaking yours?" Allow the Word of God to penetrate your heart and soul and help you in your time of need. At times it will be hard to read the Word. Read it anyway it will soothe your mind and soul. Let God search you and purge you and look into your lives and redeem you (Psalm 139:23-24; 2 Corinthians 13:5; Matthew 5:8; Ephesians 4:17-32). Develop a Godly habit of reading the Word, Praying and Praising God. Yes, praising God in the midst of the confusion and sorrow. And, be like Abraham Lincoln who said: "I believe the will of God prevails; without Him all human reliance is vain; without the assistance of that divine being I cannot succeed; (but) with that assistance I cannot fail." Take extra and excellent care of yourself. Have a positive mindset that all shall be well. Think positive thoughts towards yourself and your children. Love yourself and your children. Have a Godly response to your afflictions and be assured all shall be well. As Oswald Chambers summarized, "if I will do my duty, not for duty's sake but because I believe God is engineering my circumstances, then at the very point of my obedience all of the magnificent grace of God is mine through the glorious atonement by the Cross of Christ." Thank God that you are not defined by the circumstances or experiences that happened in your life, but by the hand of Almighty God who will make all things work together for good in your life. Obey God ! Trust God ! Yes, Almighty God, who made you and your children, says all shall be well with you and your children. It's a day of God's blessings (2 Corinthians 6:2). God will take away all your shame and humiliation that resulted from divorce. Rejoice in the Lord that you are afflicted so you can learn about God's Word and His faithfulness (Psalm 119:71-72). When you put your faith in the Living God your fears will disappear. His faithfulness reaches beyond the clouds (Psalm 36:5). When you experience fear, doubt and worry trust God and Like Our Lord and Savior proclaim: "yet not as I will, but as you will" (Matthew 26:39), and let all the glory go to your Heavenly Father. God will not allow you to fall. He will keep your steps from falling (Psalm 37:31). God will do all He said He would do (1 Thessalonians 5:24; 2 Thessalonians 3:3). He will direct your steps. God cares about all the details of your life including all the smallest details. So, don't lose heart. Be encouraged. "If you are right with God, the very thing which is an affliction to you is working out an eternal weight of glory. The afflictions may come from good people or from bad people, but behind the whole thing is God" (Oswald Chambers). So, count it all joy when you fall into afflictions (James 1:2-3). See afflictions as means to joy in the Lord. The joy of the Lord is your strength (Nehemiah 8:10). Job informed us that, man, who is born of woman is of few days and full of trouble (Job 14:1). Since our lives are connected with those of others, we sometimes suffer for the sins of foolishness, missteps and mistakes of others (1 Corinthians 12:26). We should not lose heart but cling to God who made all of us. Ensure that you do not have self-pity because victory is yours. You have Our Lord Jesus Christ by your side. He is your advocate. His grace is sufficient for you (2 Corinthians 12:9). Whatever the heartaches God has made you victorious because Jesus finished the work in Calvary. He proclaimed that "it is finished" (John 19:30). Affliction grows us in patience, allows us to have empathy for others so we can comfort them in their own time of affliction. It also grows our faith in God Almighty. It draws us closer to the throne of grace so we can obtain grace and mercy in our time of need. We develop trust in God and gain a proper perspective to help others who are suffering. Allow your response to adversity to make you and not break you. Look to God and be saved (Isaiah 45:22). Focus your mind, heart and body on Jesus Christ and your trials, difficulties and worries will be replaced with God's peace as you solely trust Him to take care of you and your children. Hope in Him and in His assurance that all shall be well (Psalm 1:1-3). Jeremiah 17 verses 7 to 8 says you are blessed because you trust in the Lord. Your hope is in Him. And that you are like a tree planted by the waters that spread out your roots by the river, and that you will not fear when heat comes because your leaf will be green. And that you will neither be anxious in the year of drought nor will you cease from yielding fruit. God uses brokenness to make us complete. Every disappointment becomes His appointment. As the Lord Our Father is compassionate and gracious ....(Psalm 103:8,10), we should be ready to show compassion and mercy to others who are going through tribulations like us. "O Lord, whenever we're afraid, we'll put our trust in You to lead, protect, and guide our way, and help us make it through" (Sper). Embrace faith and let go of worry during this time of your life. The Word of God says, "many are the afflictions of the righteous, but the Lord delivers him (and her) out of them all. He guards all his (or her) bones not one of them is broken" (Psalm 34:19-20). Learn to be careful about things you can control. And know that you are loved by your Creator who can control all you cannot control. Leave all the circumstances beyond your control to the Almighty who made heaven and earth and who made you and your children. He loves you unconditionally regardless of what you are going through and what has happened. Know what to do and have wisdom and also have faith and trust in the One who can lead you to do the right things in this situation. Open yourselves to Jesus and tell Him your hurts, sorrows and afflictions and you will be made whole by His love. Pray for God's peace in the face of turmoil and disharmony. Do not look back like Lot's wife did (Genesis 19:26; Luke 9:62). Resist the temptations to look at what was. Look forward with praise and thanksgiving to what blessings are to come into your life and to that of your offsprings. It can be hard to see beyond the sufferings and heartaches you are going through right now. But trust in the One who brought you here that all shall be well. Do not get bogged down with what is happening now, so you don't miss the opportunities and miracles that God has for you today and in the future. Paul encouraged us that he has learned to forget what is behind and look forward to what is ahead with the hope of getting the crown God has for him (Philippians 3:13-14). God can heal the wounds that others have inflicted on you purposely and unpurposely. God will use the situation to make you wiser and Godly. He will sharpen your trust in Him. God specializes in making weak vessels to become strong vessels. God creates treasures from what has been discarded and labelled rubbish by the world. He makes heroes from whimps. He will make you a Masterpiece. At the end you will be amazed at how God has transformed you. Do not despair. Do not lose hope. Your God and my God is able. He is a God of transformation. He has good plans for you (Jeremiah 29:11-13). God who brings beauty out of ashes (Jeremiah 31:4; Psalm 30:11-12;

Isaiah 61:3) will sustain you and bring beauty out of the ashes of your divorce. Because those who know God's Name trust in You God, for You Lord, have never forsaken those who seek You (Psalm 9:10). Give God, the Lord of new beginnings a chance to remake your life like a Potter who molds the dust from the scratch (Isaiah 64:8; Jeremiah 18:6; Revelation 21:5; Genesis 2:7; John 9:5-6; Isaiah 29:16; Romans 9:14-24). Place your life (the dust) in the Hands of the Potter who will remake you and your children (Jeremiah 18:1-9). It will soon be your time to laugh (Ecclesiastes 3:4). Do not argue. Do not fret. Just let the Holy Spirit guide and direct you. Waves of emotions and sufferings and afflictions may sweep over you, remember God will keep you afloat and you shall swim over them. When you pass through the waters, they shall not drown you and when you pass through fire it shall not engulf you (Isaiah 43:2). "When overwhelmed with problems, when weak or tired or ill, when storms are fierce and raging just hear His 'Peace be still' (Jarvis). God, who is able to keep you from stumbling (Jude 24), will hold you steady. When you sigh, cry, or pray He Hears your faintest cry (Psalm 38:9). Remember God loves you and He will show you kindness, love, mercy and peace (Isaiah 54:10). Your time of favor has come (Psalm 102:13). Chek Phang Hia of Our Daily Bread Ministries encouraged you that, "(your) God is greater than all of (your) troubles and Chek pointed out further that (you) should "never measure God's unlimited power by (your) limited expectations." God, Our Rock and Lord is perfect, and He is a God of justice (Deuteronomy 32:4). Your suffering will produce Godly character and embolden you with patience, hope and trust in the Lord (Romans 5:3-5; 2 Corinthians 4:17; 1 Peter 4:12-13). Remember, as David Egner of Our Daily Bread Ministries pointed out that, "the power of God within you is greater than the pressure of troubles around you." So, trust in the Lord and lean not on your own understanding and in all your ways acknowledge Him and He shall direct your paths (Proverbs 3:5-6). Trust God with your words and actions. He is not blind to your circumstances or your choices. God is all-knowing and He pays attention to every detail of our lives. He is always ready to encourage and strengthen us. All we have to do is trust Him as our faithful Father. Count your blessings. Name them one by one. This will allow you to look forward to more blessings from your Creator during this time of testing and tribulation. He is excellent and faithful. Believe me, He can be trusted because His love is unfailing and sure (Psalm 111:7; 71:3; 2 Chronicles 16:9). Be firmly planted in the Lord from now on and you will never be disappointed. Smith reiterated: "why must I bear this pain? I cannot tell; I only know my Lord does all things well. And so, I trust in God, my all in all, For He will bring me through, whate'er befall." Be patient in tribulation and know that God who has promised is faithful (Hebrews 10:23; Isaiah 41:8-16; 43:1-7). Make your relationship with God the dominating factor and focus of your life (Matthew 6:33). And do not forget the excellent things God has done for you (Psalm 103:2). God forgives all our sins, heals all our diseases, redeems our lives from death and crowns and envelopes us with His love (Psalm 103:3-4). Thank God for His provision and unfailing love for you and your children. God will make you **thrive** and not only survive (Psalm 35:27). Remember, God's faithfulness, love and compassion will shine through to you in this your time of suffering, afflictions, adversity, abandonment, bitterness, ridicule, hardship, pains and laments. Have hope because of God's great love and compassion which fails not, and which are new every morning (Lamentations 3:22-23). Endure and be blessed (James 5:11). Hang in there. Do not despair or lose hope. You become strengthened when you don't give up or lose hope. Pray for strength and the power to endure and God will turn you dreams into reality. His plans for you are excellent. You are loved and not forgotten. He will continue to order your steps because the steps of the anointed are ordained by the Lord (Psalm 37:23). Your days are ordered by Our father who loves you so so dearly. He is the architect of your life who will make all things work together for good for you and perfect all those things that concern you (Romans 8:28; Psalm 138:8a). All you need to do is trust and have faith that this too shall pass, and God will use you to be a comfort to those coming behind you (2 Corinthians 1:4) after strengthening you. Remember, that nothing is too hard for the Lord (Jeremiah 32:17 & 27) and He knows all you are going through right now. You are under God's grace today and you will be under His grace tomorrow. God will bring showers of blessings to you out of your storms of adversity. As you go through this storm, know one thing, that circumstances might get worse before it gets better like it did for the Hebrew children before Moses got them out of Egypt (Exodus 5). But praise God. His grace will sustain you and the storm will pass. It's always the darkest before the dawn. The dawn eventually breaks into daylight. Be satisfied in the Lord. Sometimes we simply need to be reminded that God is for us. That God has us covered. Psalm 33 verse 20 says that "we wait in hope for the Lord, He is our help and our shield." And Psalm 33 verse 18 reiterates that "the eyes of the Lord are on those who fear Him, on those whose hope is in His unfailing love." Do not make the joy and victory of your life dependent on your circumstances or on other people's choices. Rejoice in the Lord and trust in His holy name and might, not in warhorse or an armor (Psalm 33:16-17). Aim high, expect God's best and always be ready and willing to give God your best (2 Peter 1:5-7). And as you trust in God, His plans which is always the best will unfold in your lives. His thoughts are not your thoughts, neither are your ways His ways, declares the Lord (Isaiah 55:8). But know one thing: He has excellent plans for your future (Jeremiah 29:11-13).

Deal with the anger constructively and in a Godly way

ROMANS 12 VERSE 19 says we should allow God to fight for us. Let go and let God take excellent care of you and He will neither leave you nor forsake you (Deuteronomy 31:6 & 8). He will take care of everything in your life. Believe me. He cares. He takes care of the downtrodden and the forgotten. God is good (Nahum 1:7). Trust God in the storms and He will give you the peace that passes all understanding and calm you amidst the turbulent of anger and different emotions spurting out every moment. Turn all the emotions to God. Remember, you will embody lots of anger. There will be anger at God, different groups of people, some of who are judgemental, anger at your former spouse, some friends and family members and even the world at large. You will feel alone, isolated and frustrated. Cry on your Papa's shoulders after the children are in bed. Let God know how you feel. Believe me it helps. It is catharsis. If you have the time and the money talk to a Christian counselor who will guide you with the Word of God and prayers. Work on codependency, emotional insecurities, neediness, manipulations, controlling and any other attitudes that might have been cultivated by you or others as a result of your relationship with your former spouse. Stay close to true, trustworthy friends and relatives. Avoid those who act as Judge, Jury and Executioners to divorced individuals. Believe me, you will come across so many of them in your time of ordeal. Avoid those who profess that God hate divorce and therefore hates you. Know this, as I said before, God hates divorce, but loves those who are divorced. Do not let people hold you accountable and guilty for what happened in your marriage. Most of the time if you attend a God-ordained church, your pastor can be a source of help during this trying-times. Stay close to those who embrace and do not snub, ignore or avoid you. Look for support, resources and in divorce support groups within your church. Start one if there is none in your church. You will be surprised to see it become a source of help to different groups of people, those who are divorced and their children. Let out your anger as you talk about your feelings. Read the Word of God. Cherish them and memorize some passages with your children. These will aid you as you combat criticisms and back-biting from critics and those who will like to put you down or make you feel "less-than." Please note that some former friends will take sides. Be ready for this and do not be angered by this fact. Always know that we are all human and individuals are different. Individuals are also entitled to their own opinions. Always cherish the fact that God loves you and your children and take that to the Bank of Jesus trust. Stay faithful to God despite pressure and discouragement. This will be helpful, and it will inspire other people to give God the glory (Daniel 6:19-28). After Daniel's divine deliverance from the lion's den, the king gave all the glory to Daniel's God as the Almighty. Those who notice your faithfulness and unwavering devotion to God will praise His Name and give Him glory. So, stay focused on your

Papa and He will see you through your ordeal and sufferings. You will graduate with flying colors as His child.

Forgive, Forgive, Try to Forget, Move on with this your one God-given life

THIS PHASE IS THE most difficult. Job was able to look at his problems from Godly perspective and he gave God the ultimate control of his situation in Job 1 verse 21 when he said, "naked I came from my mother's womb, and naked shall I return, the Lord gave and the Lord has taken away Blessed be the name of the Lord." Ask the Lord to make you look at things from Job and Joseph's perspective when things are hard. Learn about mercy, grace and forgiveness from God and from the Word of God. Because Jesus forgave you fully, forgive all those that have sinned against you (Matthew 5:44). Heed Jesus' advice to forgive those who hurt us seventy times seven (Matthew 18:21-22). This act of forgiveness will free your soul, mind and body from the stress of unforgiveness and inner turmoil or anger. God will take excellent care of you and your children if you are blessed with them.

If you want to get your blessings from God, you will need to forgive to gain back your sanity. This is a long process especially if you have been unfairly treated. It is only after you forgive that you can start to heal and live a wholistic lifestyle and get your blessings from God and **thrive**. Believe me, God will pour blessings into your life and your children's. So, let go, forgive and let God take the reins of your life from now on. It has worked for others it will work for you. Joseph told his brothers: you meant evil against me, but God turned it to good (Genesis 50:20). Have the same mindset and be greatly blessed and have life in abundance (John10:10). Do not let unforgiveness steal your joy and rob you of your blessings. Someone said that choosing not to forgive somebody is like eating poison and expecting the other person to die. So do not let unforgiving heart rob you of all the blessings God has in store for you. Learn to let go and be at peace with the past. Remember one thing, if someone does not want to be in your life, God will help you deal with that fact. But you need to learn to let them go. Abram let Lot go and He was blessed (Genesis 13:5-13). Naomi let Orpah go and she and Ruth were blessed (Ruth 1). So, learn to leave those who do not want to be part of your life go and get your blessings. Moses let go of his Pharaoh upbringing and he became useful to God in leading the Israelites out of Egypt (Exodus 5 & 6). God will put Godly people in your life that needs to be there for you and help you move forward to holistic health. Jesus died to provide all of us with forgiveness. We should follow His example by forgiving all those who sin against us. As Jesus loved others including those unlovable, we should also love others (1 John 4:19; John 13:34-35). Let go of bitterness and open your hearts to forgiveness as Jesus did (Luke 23:34). Do not rob yourself of joy through having an anxiety about the future. Rejoice in God's character even when circumstances are uncertain. Cast your cares and anxieties on God because He cares for you (1 Peter 5:7). Pray for and gain a heart of wisdom (Psalm 90:12) as you look forward to your future that is full of hope. Stay focused on Godly things and things that have eternal values. Berg advised us that, "day by day and with each passing moment, strength I find to meet my trials here; trusting in my Father's wise bestowment, I've no cause for worry or for fear." So, go forth into your future with confidence without fretting or worrying in the bosom of your Almighty Papa. Forgive as the Lord forgives you (Colossians 3:13). Live in the peace and joy of God's forgiveness (John 14:27). "But above all these things put on love which is the bond of perfection. And whatever you do in word or deed, do all in the name of the Lord Jesus giving thanks to God the Father through Him" (Colossians 3:14 &17). Always remember to have boundaries and discernment too and be as wise as a serpent and as gentle as a dove (Matthew 10:16).

Moving on with your life: Remarriage or remaining single?

THIS IS A DIFFICULT decision that must be made. Weigh all your options, pray and seek God's will.

When He has tried you, you shall come forth as gold (Job 23:10). Shine brightest as God's Masterpiece. Remember that God has all things under control regarding your life. Trust God with your life and your children's life because He sees the big picture. God knows what you do not know. "In all things at all times having all that you need" (2 Corinthians 9:8). Our God shall supply all your needs according to His riches in glory in Christ Jesus (Philippians 4:19) Amen. Sow into God's kingdom as you can and be assured you will reap what you sow in due course. If you don't have money sow your time and other things that you have into God's kingdom. Read the Word, Pray, Praise, and be in communion with genuine Godly Christians. I mean those who will not judge you. Do not rush into making decisions. Seek God's face. The Holy Spirit will lead you in your choice and you will not be disappointed. Take time for God, yourself and for your children. Pray and plan for a future that will ensure independence for you and your children. Do not base the plan for your future on anything except on God. He will surprise you. He never fails or disappoints His children. God loves you and your children. Make God the center of your life to gain fulfilment from sufferings, trials and tribulations. Love Jesus first and all the love of your life will follow amicably (2 Peter 1: 5 & 7). For without Him you cannot find joy and love. Sheridan Voysey of Our Daily Bread Ministries reiterated that "without God as our center, life's pleasures and sorrows lead only to disillusionment." Solomon advised that without God there is no enjoyment in anything (Ecclesiastes 2:26). If you choose to remarry be cautious and do not be unequally yoked with unbelievers (2 Corinthians 6:14). Be careful. Do not rush into relationships. Be prayerful and seek your Father's face as you look for a mate that will be your best friend and your children's role model. Make sure you choose a Godly mate that respects you and your children. And if you sense that God has called you to be single, use your time wisely to aid God's ministry and fulfill your time here on earth by serving and using your God-given gifts to help others and make life comfortable for you and your children. Believe me God will use you. He will not disappoint you. If you have time and talent, go back to school or learn a trade. This will prove helpful to you and your children. You will become a role model for your children and others too. In any way do all you do to glorify God and He will smile on you and bless you and your household. "Delight yourself also in the Lord, And He shall give you the desires of your heart" (Psalm 37:4). Remember that you are more than conquerors through Jesus Christ who loves you (Romans 8:37). God will also lead you to triumph (2 Corinthians 2:14). All the promises of God for you are Yes and Amen in Him to the glory of God in your life (2 Corinthians 1:20). Do not forget to do everything with thanksgiving to your Creator who will make all grace abound towards you (Colossians 3:17), and ensure that no man can stand before you all the days of your life (Joshua 1:5) because you are His blood-bought child. This Lord who loves you will establish you and guard you from the evil one (2 Thessalonians 3:3). So, do not fear. Move forward in your Papa's Name and choose what the Holy Spirit inspires you to do. And your faithful Father will do what is best in your life (1 Thessalonians 5:24) because His faithfulness reaches to the clouds (Psalm 36:5) and all over the world. Focus and fix your eyes on God. He will surprise you with His blessings and with answers to your prayers. The reason why many of us fail is because we trade what we want most, which is God Himself, for what we want now. Please God most. Don't settle for less or crumbs instead of the real loaf. Pursue God. Stay close to God by looking at the Cross of Calvary. Avoid impulsivity. Remember, the greater the challenge, trial and tribulation, the greater the reward. Let me leave you with the song by Hillsong United artist: "I will never be the same again. I can never return, I've closed the door. I will walk the path, I'll run the race. And I will never be the same again. Fall like fire, soak like rain. Flow like mighty waters, again and again. Sweep away the darkness, burn away the chaff. And let a flame burn to glorify Your Name. There are higher heights, there are deeper seas. Whatever you need to do, Lord do in me. The glory of God fills my life. And I will never be the same again." Sing this song over and over again and strive not to be the same again. Aspire to be a new creation in Jesus Christ and your life will take a turn for the best. Believe me, God brings jewels out of those lives others regard to as "abandoned and discarded life." Lord gives us the courage to face an unknown future. Amy Boucher Pye of Our Daily Bread Ministries reiterated that, "when we wear the rags of 'ashes,' He gently gives us a coat of praise." Amy continued that God's faithfulness allows us to realize that God is "willing and able to turn our grief to dancing once again and give us sufficient grace in this life and full joy in heaven." Psalm 30 verse 11 pointed out that God turns our mourning into dancing. Isaiah 61 verse 3 says, "to console those who mourn in Zion, to give them beauty for ashes. The oil of joy for mourning. The garment of praise for the spirit of heaviness. That they may be called trees of righteousness. The planting of the Lord, that He may be glorified." Remember, God will neither leave you nor forsake you (Deuteronomy 31:6&8), because you are special. You are the planted tree of righteousness. So, cast all your anxiety on God because He cares for you (1 Peter 5:7). This truth, sure should give you comfort, assurance, hope, strength and courage to face each day with fortitude and faith and embrace the future with confidence. Generously give your time, talent, gifts and efforts to advance God's Kingdom and you will be able to embrace your God-endowed destiny. I leave you with Sper's encouraging words that says: "when you are afraid of what's ahead, remember, God is near, He'll give you strength and joy and hope and calm your inner fear."

Conclusion: Life goes on ! Even after the divorce !! Believe me life does go on !!!

NOW THAT YOU HAVE had some time to peruse the book *Thriving After Divorce*, one thing should be clear to you: You are justified. God loves you and your children dearly. Because you are justified, God declares you righteous because of the shed blood of Jesus Christ. Stand by faith. You are justified. God declares you innocent of any crime or guilt. Since you were bought with a precious blood of the Lamb, go around with your head high. No matter what anyone says, you are a Masterpiece (Ephesians 2:10). You are special. You are God's jewel (Malachi 3: 16-17; Zechariah 9:16). Whatever has happened in your life does not make you "less-than." You are as precious as any other person whatever their marital status. Do not let anyone smear you with condemnation or guilt of any kind. God does not hate you or your children. You are not "second-hand" individuals. You are gifts. You are God's gifts to the world. So, utilize what you learn from your afflictions to help those around you because you are blessed and highly favored. Your divorce was not caused because of your inadequacy or imperfectness. This should make you shout Halleluia !

I leave you with the promise of the Lord to you as one who is divorced, in Isaiah 54 verses 5 to 8 which proclaims, "like a woman (or man) forsaken and grieved in spirit, like a youthful wife (or husband) when you were refused says your God, for a mere moment I have forsaken you. But with great mercies I will gather you. With a little wrath I hid my face from you for a moment. But with everlasting kindness I will have mercy on you. Says the Lord your Redeemer." And also, verses 10 to 13 of Isaiah 54 that says, "For the mountain shall depart and the hills be removed, but my kindness shall not depart from you, nor shall my convenant of peace be removed (from you) says the Lord, who has mercy on you. O you afflicted one, tossed with tempest, and not comforted, behold I will lay your stones with colorful gems and lay your foundations with sapphires. I will make your pinnacles of rubies, your gates of crystal, and all your walls of precious stones. All your children shall be taught by the Lord and great shall be the peace of your children." Praise God ! Be blessed !!

www.ingramcontent.com/pod-product-compliance
Lightning Source LLC
Chambersburg PA
CBHW061514040426
42450CB00008B/1615